CONTENTS

FOREWORD

A NOTE FROM THE AUTHOR.

A wonderful way to use this book is to begin it on the first day of any month, and continue for 30 days (there is an extra day included for those months with 31 days), and begin again for every month thereafter.

However, it is really up to you how you would like to work with it. You can start on any day and work ahead from there for 30 days in a row, or read it on those days when you feel drawn and are in need of some inspiration, by choosing any piece that may call out to you. If you are really up for it, you could even devour it all in one sitting.

How you work with this material is not important, what's important is that you do so in any way that feels right for you. It is my deepest desire and fondest intention that this book makes a difference in your life and that you are truly blessed by it.

Love and blessings, Veronica Hay

DEDICATION

I dedicate this book to every soul who has ever searched for the answers to life's greatest mysteries.

To every mortal who has wandered, struggled, floundered, and fallen.

To every child who has ever felt lost, alone, and abandoned.

To every heart that has ever been broken, and every spirit that has ever been crushed.

To everyone who has ever had the courage to feel the pain, the sadness, the disappointments, really feel them and move through to the other side of light, love, and absolute joy.

To every individual who believed in the impossible and made it happen.

To every mystic who tasted the sweet nectar of something more and told of it.

To every being who has triumphed and forged ahead victorious.

To every person who made the choice to keep on dancing.

To all the actors on my stage, who came here to play with me.

I dedicate this book to YOU!

INTRODUCTION

Today, I wish for you ...

What if, when you opened your eyes in the morning, the first thing you saw was your fairy godmother, or an angel, or your higher self, or a celestial being, or someone you love who always has your best interest at heart? What if they had been waiting for you to awaken, just so they could tell you what they had in store for you today?

What if, instead of rushing out the door with a cup of coffee and a mind full of worry and negative expectations, you took a few moments to allow this being to help you start your day?

What if they wanted to fill your mind with the most beautiful thoughts and infuse your being with infinite possibilities of what might happen if you were open to let it all in?

Would it put a smile on your face to know happiness is only a moment away? That today, someone had your back and wanted the best for you. Would you feel good about your next day as you lay down to sleep each evening?

Would you wonder what they would say today, that might inspire you, comfort you, make you think, cause you to laugh, ease your burdens, open your heart, and motivate you to move forward with your dreams? What if they offered you a new way of looking at the world, outside the box, or made you feel you were given a nice warm hug of encouragement for today?

What if, simply by absorbing their words of daily inspiration, you were transported to a magical place where anything was possible?

Well, for the next 30 days, I will be that someone, if you let me. It will be my honor, my joy, my reason for being to offer you the world, at least in the form of - Today, I Wish For You.

It is a scientific fact that we are all connected, and whatever our intention is for ourselves and for another is a powerful thing. This book was written with YOU in mind. Yes, you, the person reading these words right now.

 "Every morning you have two choices: continue to sleep with your dreams or wake up and chase them."

— CARMELO ANTHONY

So, what are our plans for today? Perhaps we will state a declaration or decree to possibly create some free money or read a powerful blessing to help manifest more abundance and prosperity into our lives? Maybe we'll enjoy delicious afternoon tea together at 3 o'clock or indulge in some decadent chocolate with zero calories.

Possibly, we may become a silent angel for another soul and spread random acts of kindness wherever we go. We could watch with amazement, as a lady bug takes flight in a way we had never noticed before, or we could create something new to give to the world. On another day, we could shower ourselves with appreciation for all that we are or give up the shoulds and the woulds and the coulds and do something different, something that shakes us up and rocks our world.

How about letting our imagination soar, setting our passion free, or resting in this precious, timeless moment, experiencing the real power of now? Let's make a wish for ourselves and a person we love and send it out into the world, or listen to a guided audio meditation, or choose to be happy for no reason. Is it finally time to believe that anything is possible?

It is all here for you. Waiting...

Will you join me? Will you take your place beside me?

Will you answer the call, hear the whisper, say yes to the magic, dance with the wonder, allow in the miracles? Will you?

Well, let's get started.

DAY 1 - AN ABUNDANCE BLESSING

TODAY, I WISH FOR YOU, A BLESSING OF ABUNDANCE.

May the clouds break and the heavens pour down upon you more joy, more love, more laughter, and more money than you could have ever dreamed of.

May the sun shine its golden light of prosperity through every cell of your extraordinary body.

May you be cleansed today of any resistance or feelings of unworthiness you may still be holding onto.

May your false illusions of doubt, fear and scarcity gently fall away like soft white feathers on a gentle breeze.

May you be willing, simply willing, to allow the Universe to shower you with miracles today.

May the angels wrap you in their shining wings of opulence.

May the fairies deliver you to their pot of gold at the end of a majestic rainbow.

May your eyes shine with the glorious truth of who you really are and may that truth uplift others in your presence to their own inner knowing.

May your ears hear the sound of perfection ringing in your soul.

May you taste the deliciousness of every precious bite of life as your day unfolds moment by moment with amazing grace, heartfelt love, and a bounty of magnificent money.

As this day ends, may you slumber, wrapped in an exquisite blanket of enduring peace and profound gratitude.

May the last words you speak today be: Thank you!

DAY 2 - THAT SOMEONE IS ME

That someone is me ...

TODAY, I WISH FOR YOU TO KNOW THAT:

Someone is lighting a candle for you and holding you in the light of that flame which burns brightly for you.

Someone is feeling your pain, your grief, and your sorrow today, and transforming it into joy, serenity, and love.

Someone is thinking kindly of you today and blessing your life with empowering words and grand visions of your finest achievements waiting to be born. They are honored to hold your desires for you, even when you may lose sight of them. Marvel in that and feel empowered by it.

Someone is imagining you today surrounded by angels, spirits, healing energies, starlight, magic, and wonder. Wrap yourself in all of that.

Someone is understanding today, the depths of what you have been going through, and is embracing you with deep compassion and trusting in your own profound inner knowing to see you through.

Someone is holding your hand today and letting you know you are never alone and never have been, even though there have been moments when you lost your way and felt abandoned and afraid.

Someone truly knows today, perhaps at a level you do not yet, that all is well, even though it may not appear to be so. You are here in all your splendor and there is great meaning and purpose in your life. Without you, nothing would be the same for any of us. Know that and be inspired by it.

Someone is nurturing your dreams today and keeping them close as they evolve, expand and flourish. Be excited about that and claim them.

Someone is praying for you today and their prayers are being heard and answered.

Someone is whispering gently to you today to keep going no matter what, one day at a time, one step at a time, one inch at a time. We are all celebrating that you haven't given up and that you are making such an immense difference for all of us.

Someone is enfolding you in the light today as things in your world seem to be falling apart, and putting them back together for you, in new, miraculous, and astonishing ways. Trust and believe in that.

Feel the love, cherish the knowing, drink in the joy, and take comfort and strength in all of it.

4

It is right here waiting for you. Reach for it. Embrace it. Know it is yours.

DAY 3 - SUCCULENT, MELT IN YOUR MOUTH, TO DIE FOR, CHOCOLATE

TODAY, I WISH FOR YOU:

Doors opening widely and invitingly, where they had been previously closed, and shut.

Sincere compliments from beguiling strangers, who might end up being friends.

Unexpected, delightful money - coins, cash, bank notes, legal tender.

Succulent, melt in your mouth, to die for, chocolate.

Fascinating, riveting conversation.

Your favorite outfit on sale for 90% off.

Your winning numbers finally showing up.

A good hair day.

Warm, soft, sweet smiles that tickle your heart.

Enough laughter to make your sides ache.

All green lights along your way.

Intriguing winks from a captivating admirer across a crowded room.

Everyone gladly and most respectfully moving aside for you as you move about your world.

Opportunities appearing from out of nowhere, ripe and ready to embark upon.

That certain someone you have been thinking about, calling you out of the blue.

A lost and cherished possession unexpectedly returning to you.

A chance encounter with a kind and generous benefactor.

A secret from your past revealing changes in your life for the better.

The innocent wish you made upon a star or put under your pillow all those years ago, coming true now.

A FREE latte, with lots of whipped cream on top. (*Don't forget to wipe your nose off after this one.*)

Something amazing in your email that causes you to kiss your computer.

A handwritten, embellished, and beautiful letter, in your mailbox.

Extra long cuddles, hugs, and kisses from the beloved, furry creatures in your life.

Taking the first step, (perhaps trembling just a little), toward a long, forgotten dream.

A text message so exciting, that you can't put your phone down all day.

The answer to your most heartfelt prayer.

A person in your life who makes you glad you got up this morning.

Last, but not least, an astonishing MIRACLE!

DAY 4 - WHAT A LADYBUG CAN TEACH YOU ABOUT LIFE

TODAY, I WISH FOR YOU, A DAY OF MAGIC.

Most people love ladybugs. Being blessed enough to have a ladybug land on you or in your garden can be a magical moment. Many insects may pose a threat but ladybugs are harmless and beneficial. That's why so many of us cherish them and even believe they bring good luck. Well, that and because they are so damn cute!

This morning I watched a 27-second video of a ladybug getting ready to fly. It astounded me and I was deeply touched at the elaborate way this tiny creature folded its wings to tuck them away.

At that moment I realized how much of life we are not aware of, how many miracles abound that are seen by the human eye as an everyday occurrence. These everyday miracles exist all around us if only we have the eyes to see them. It made me vow to be more on the lookout for what the Universe has been wanting to show me. Instead of focusing so much on what appears to be worries and conflicts in my day, I can open my eyes, my mind, and my heart to the treasures before me.

So, today I wish for you to experience something magical and find joy and delight in that.

You can watch the 27-second ladybug video below. That would be a good place to start. Then ask yourself what wisdom little Miss Ladybug has to offer you. You may be surprised by what this darling little creature has to share with you.

Scientists Sneak A Peek At How Ladybugs Fold Their Wings
http://n.pr/2q58yHS

DAY 5 - MIRACLES ARE THE ORDER OF YOUR DAY

TODAY, I WISH FOR YOU:

Less pain in your life and more peace.

Less sorrow and more joy.

Less worry and more hope.

Less struggle and more victory.

Less fear and more love.

Less disappointment and more dreams coming true.

TODAY, I WISH:

That your day overflows with insights, inspirations, aha moments, and dazzling breakthroughs.

That you let go of the false illusions that still hold you captive and embrace the divinity that stirs in your soul.

That your prayers be answered today, one after another, and your wishes be delivered in the arms of the angels.

That you laugh for no reason today, and play with no purpose.

That you be the gift you already are today for yourself, for another, and for the world.

Instead of shortages and scarcity today, that you be showered with compliments, kindness, and an avalanche of golden crisp money.

That you experience abundance as you never have before and hold it in your heart where the treasures reside always.

Instead of problems and difficulties today, that your moments be filled with ease and brilliant solutions.

That seemingly wrong turns on your path today, be blessed with amazing opportunities and dark clouds clear all around you to reveal their delightful silver linings.

That you discover today that the wonders of the world are inside you and ponder why it took you so long to find them.

That you be shocked today at what is possible, awakened to the extraordinary, and stunned by the magic of it all.

That you see where you had been blind.

That you heal where you had been sick.

That you understand where you had been confused.

That you know your purpose, rejoice in it, and, finally, give it to the world.

That miracles be the order of your day today and from this day forward.

That you sleep tonight with a fairy on your pillow and wake up with a new song in your beautiful heart.

DAY 6 - THE MAN WITH THE MUSTACHE

TODAY, I WISH FOR YOU:

To remember the people, places, and simple things along your journey each day that make such a difference in your life when you are fully aware of their presence.

I would like to share a story that may help illustrate what I am talking about so that you may begin to see whom and what you have to be grateful for.

THE MAN WITH THE MUSTACHE

I saw him today! I haven't seen him for awhile, but I saw him today, in that same seat on the bus, where I've seen him for the past 17 years. The man with the mustache.

He looked a little older, a bit tired perhaps, but the same. In a world filled with so many changes, I find it comforting when I see him, like an old shoe that is always there somewhere under the bed and reappears from time to time.

Over the years, I have wondered about him, who he is, where he gets off the bus, what his name is, and what his life is like. Not once, in all those years, have we spoken or even acknowledged one another, and yet every time I see him I wonder about his world.

I wonder in the last 17 years if he has fallen in or out of love. I wonder if he wakes up at four o'clock in the morning, thinking about life. I wonder if he has children, if he lives alone, what he likes on his pizza, what he takes in his coffee, what his dreams are. I wonder if the years have been kind to him or if they have taken their toll.

He has a serious, chiseled kind of face, which makes me think he must do a serious kind of work, not an artist or a painter, but an engineer or a geologist.

He looks like a person who analyzes a lot and sits in meaningful contemplation. I wonder how I would feel if he moved away, and I didn't see him on the bus anymore. I'm sure I would, after a time, wonder what happened to him, what turn in the road his life has taken.

It's funny, even though we've never met or spoken in all these years, he makes me feel less alone, just by being there. I feel touched by him. In a way, our souls have met. For a few moments, we've shared time and space, traveled down the same road, however short, on our way to somewhere.

Isn't that all we do with people anyway, for a short while, travel down the same road, share time and space, on our way to somewhere?

The world is full of people who make us feel less alone. I wonder if they know it. The stranger on the bus, the girl who cuts your hair, the fellow who takes your order at your favorite restaurant, the cashier at the grocery store. We all have something in common; we're all in this together.

Still, we place such little importance on these events, sometimes even walking around in a daze, oblivious to all of it, on our way to somewhere else, waiting for the bigger moments in life, you know, the ones that really matter.

And yet, these bigger moments are so few and last for such a little while.

Perhaps if we thought of these simple times as flowers, and instead of a huge bouquet every once in a while, we picked a daisy here, a lily there, and a rose somewhere else.

At the end of the day or week, we could look at the arrangement we've created, simply by being present, and savor the sweetness, smell the fragrance, and water the memories.

Then, at the end of our life, if we're really lucky, we might have an entire garden, to take with us into eternity.

DAY 7 - WHAT IF YOU ARE THE ONE WE'VE BEEN WAITING FOR?

MY WISH, DEAR ONE, FOR YOU TODAY, IS THAT YOU:

Bask in wealth and mellow in riches.

Bathe in love and revel in appreciation.

Rejoice in prosperity and wallow in money.

Delight in opulence and indulge in the miracle of your own soul.

I wish that today, you awaken to your brilliance, open to your own power, and claim your birthright.

I wish that you celebrate all your victories, from your smallest successes to your grandest accomplishments, with the same exuberance and heartfelt revelry.

I wish that you step fully into being today, what you imagine yourself to be, giving attention to your greatest desires and fondest intentions, all the while staying focused in this precious, timeless moment.

I wish that you set yourself free today, free of your perceived conflicts, frustrations and illusions of lack, looking fear in the face without flinching, and emerging unchained, unfettered, and unshackled.

I wish that you understand how significant you are, in the bigger scheme of things and know from the deepest place, that without you, nothing would be the same here.

I wish that your contributions to life return to you a thousandfold and you appreciate the immense difference you have already made in this world, simply by being you.

I wish that you relax in the knowing everything will be all right; you are safe, cherished, and loved beyond measure.

I wish that you release the struggle once and for all and relinquish the drama you seem so attached to, placing no importance on the illusion and every attention to the truth that, you are powerful, celebrated and held in highest regard by a beloved universe who is watching your every move, without judgment, though perhaps with some laughter, cheering you on, on this playing field we call earth.

YOU HAVE BEEN INVITED TO THE GRAND BALLROOM OF LIFE.

You are the honored guest. Come, sit at the head table. Before you lies a cornucopia of delights which pale by comparison to the treasures inside you. You need only let go and be free.

Step up to the podium and announce yourself! Why are you here and what have you chosen to add to the tapestry? What gifts will you bestow upon us that only you can give?

For every time you say yes to your dreams, the angels quiver in delight.

Every time you move forward toward a goal, your unseen friends begin to dance.

Every time you fall down and pick yourself up, the entire universe falls in reverence at your feet.

You are a light unto the world, and when you shine that light, the world is brighter. When you do it for you, you do it for everyone, because you are everyone.

What if you are the one we've been waiting for to change the world?

What if?

DAY 8 - GENEROSITY OF SPIRIT

TODAY, I WISH FOR YOU TO:

Be generous with your time.

Stay fully present with each encounter, as if this moment, is the most important, and nothing else exists.

Be generous with your words.

Never miss an opportunity to tell someone how you feel about them, or something they have done. A word of encouragement, a note of appreciation, or a sincere compliment, can brighten someone's day and even change a life.

Be generous with your thoughts.

Think the best of others, and see them as they would like to be, and not as they are now.

Be generous with your money.

Find an occasion to share what you have. Money is like love: the more you give away, the more returns to you.

Be generous with your heart.

Keep it open, no matter how frightening that may be sometimes. An open heart will heal every ailment and restore peace to your spirit.

Be generous with your smile.

Offer it gladly to everyone you meet, and watch the world reflected back to you, in joyous celebration.

Be generous with your love.

It is who you are, and why you came here, and it is all that matters in the end.

DAY 9 - YOU ARE ONE IN SEVEN BILLION

Today, I wish that you choose to be happy for no reason except you are here and alive and you claim this moment as your own. It's yours. It's got your name on it. Think about this: with over 7 billion people on the planet, there isn't another person who is exactly like you. You are one in 7 billion! A magnificent, unique, shining star in this great galaxy of life!

Today, I wish that you take the child in you out to play. Step in mud puddles, get your feet wet, eat cotton candy, blow bubbles, plan a picnic, talk to strangers. Go to the park and have someone push you on the swings or climb on the monkey bars. Be silly and don't give a damn about what people think of you. Have you forgotten how much fun being silly can be?

Today, I wish that you close your eyes and imagine you are visited by your fairy godmother who wants to grant you your fondest wish.

Never mind, that you are put out about where she has been all this time. Contemplate what your wish would be. Pretend you have it now. Savor every detail. Really get into it with all the flavor and sound you can muster *(whoop, moan, yelp)* - you get the picture. *(Nobody's watching and I won't tell anyone you're actually doing this. Hey, you can trust me!)*

If you were King or Queen of the world just for today, who would you pick to be in your kingdom and why? Who would you put in the slammer? *(You may be given some good insight here into what's lurking inside you and maybe even heal something.)* But don't sweat it. You want to enjoy your day, don't you? So lighten up.

Today, I wish that you talk less and say more, taste more and eat less, appreciate more and complain less, accept more and judge less, forgive more and blame less, ultimately do nothing and allow everything.

Today, I wish that you won't do your laundry unless you absolutely have to, or the world might end.

Today, I wish that you eat *(no, devour)* something you love, something that you have denied yourself for a very long time. Think of today as a special occasion and indulge yourself *(without the guilt)*, and even smack your lips *(simply for effect)*. That's a demand. Okay, an order. Okay, an appeal. Okay, a request. Okay, maybe just a nudge...

Today, I wish that you be kind to those parts of your body you dislike. They occupy the same space as you, so you might as well make friends with them. They need love as much as you do, so show them some appreciation. *(P.S. It's good for your health.)*

Today, I wish that you say no, to something you don't want to do but feel you have to do it. You hate doing it, and you are not doing it, (unless it's a life or death thing), at least for today. Instead, say yes, to something you've always wanted to do, dreamed of doing, would give your first born child for, would walk on hot coals for, but have a thousand excuses why you could not allow yourself that much joy.

Making this choice will help you feel a lot lighter, but you may want to lie down for this one.

Enjoy your day, and make friends with some of the 7 billion people who decided to join you here at this amazing time on the planet. Get to know a few of them. Reach out and touch a heart or two, celebrate your differences, acknowledge how alike you are, where it matters. Play fair. Be nice. It really is a small world but there is room for all of us. Move over. I think I'll join you.

DAY 10- CONTEMPLATE THIS TODAY

TODAY, I WISH THAT YOU CONTEMPLATE THE FOLLOWING:

Will someone change their mind today about what is possible, because of your presence on their path, however brief that may have been?

Will someone forgive something or someone else today because of your own willingness to do so and be an inspiration and example for them?

Will someone decide not to leave the planet today because your smile or tender touch might be that one simple thing that saves their hopeless and weary heart from giving up?

Will someone think twice about getting even, or hurting another today, because you showed them the higher road?

Will someone smile sweetly tonight as they close their eyes in gentle slumber because during the day today, you made them feel like they mattered?

Contemplate this today

Will your encouragement and support help someone today come out of hiding, whatever that may be about, because you coaxed them with tiny bread crumbs scattered upon their path wrapped in love and acceptance?

If someone cries out to you today in grief and pain, will you hear them and answer, even though there is no sound to hear or tears to see? Will you acknowledge and comfort them in their silence?

Do not be fooled by appearances. Look beneath the trappings and the finery. What you find there may surprise you if you take the time to see. Move closer.

We may never know how our presence affects another walking beside us on this journey or how much of a gift we might be to all whom we encounter. Contemplate this today!

You are a living, breathing miracle and it is no accident you are here now at this auspicious time. You are the one we have been waiting for and it is time to come out and play. There is plenty of room in the sandbox!

DAY 11 - SPIRITUAL GIFTS FROM THE SOUL

TODAY, I WISH TO GIVE YOU THE FOLLOWING GIFTS FROM THE SOUL.

Please take some time to imagine yourself receiving each gift and tucking them away safely in your heart.

I give you twenty rivers with twenty different songs, the romance of a flower and a bee, the rapture of a sun-kissed face.

I give you a thousand diamonds on a sandy beach, a million emeralds in a mountain valley, a hundred rubies in a field of roses, and seven sapphires in a true blue sea.

I give you shamrocks to wish on, buttercups to dance on, tulips to cry with, and lilies to die with.

I give you trees to talk to, and meadows to hold you tight.

I give you puppy dog's noses and polar bear hugs, a unicorn's laughter, and a baby's face.

I give you moonbeams to light your way, starlight to mark your path, and soft white clouds to wrap around your heart.

I give you smiles to remind you and laughter to surround you.

I give you thunder to wake you, lightning to shake you, solitude to remake you, and music to take you to places of long ago and far away.

I give you the earth to embrace you, raindrops to taste you, friendships to mold you, and firelight to enfold you.

I give you an enchanted forest where the dreamer sleeps and waits for you.

I give you eternity in a moment and a lifetime of forevers.

I give you spring to awaken your spirit, and summer to warm your soul.

I give you autumn to wait in solitude, and winter to rest in a blanket of snow.

I give you imagination to explore, appreciation to be at your side, and magic to be your guide.

I give you Yesterday, tucked in yellow blankets of daffodils to cherish the memories each petal holds.

I give you Today, held on the wings of a butterfly, opened for the first time, to flights of fancy wherever they may be.

I give you Tomorrow, wrapped in silver mist, to be seen with the eyes of a child, heard with the ears of a fawn, and felt with the heart of a God.

I give you all the king's horses and all the king's men, and Humpty Dumpty put back together again. I give you another chance, another day, another way.

I give you all these gifts, already placed in your heart, to be opened one by one.

Whenever you are ready, they await you...

To listen to a guided audio meditation of "Gifts From the Soul" visit this link: http://geni.us/Evhak

DAY 12 - A FEW END-OF-THE-DAY QUESTIONS FOR YOU

TODAY, I WISH FOR YOU TO BE ABLE TO ANSWER YES, TO AT LEAST SOME, IF NOT ALL OF THESE QUESTIONS, BEFORE YOUR HEAD HITS THE PILLOW TONIGHT.

Did I make someone giggle, smile, or laugh today?

Did I take the time to really listen to someone today, with rapt attention, as if nothing else mattered in that precious moment but the words they spoke and the look in their eyes?

Did I allow myself to focus on all the blessings in my life today instead of contemplating the things I don't have?

Did I take a moment to imagine what I would like to experience, knowing that in the imagining is the living, and in the living, comes the joy and delight?

Did I let go today of any resentments and unforgivingness I have been holding onto, all the while realizing another person may be wounded too and struggling with their own pain?

Did I keep my word today, no matter how simple a promise I may have made, knowing it meant a lot to someone else?

Did I make a conscious choice to be happy today, no matter what is happening in my own life, for the next moment, and the next moment, and the next?

Did I stop caring about what other people think of me and give myself permission to be who I am regardless of their good opinion of me or not? Did I set myself free today by doing that?

Was I successful in noticing and appreciating the bounty before me wherever I went or was I too busy or lost in my own thoughts to notice?

Did I contribute something beautiful to the world today? A poem, a dinner, a song, an invention, a picture, a dance?

Was I kind today to anyone or anything that crossed my path, no matter how trivial or how monumental? Did I give away my heart?

Is one person richer today, because of my presence on the planet, my essence, or my decision to keep on going no matter what?

Did I learn something new today, something about life, something about myself, or something about another I didn't know before?

Did I let go of my attachment to being right today, and open my mind to the possibility of another way, without judgment?

Will someone sleep better tonight because of me? Will they awaken in the morning believing in themselves again and walk with their head held high?

Was I the answer to someone's prayers today?

If today was to be my last day on the planet, would I feel happy about how I lived it?

DAY 13 - WILL YOU?

Sometimes when we move forward in life toward a very big dream, it may feel like too much of a leap in consciousness for us to hold all by ourselves. It is at those times that we need to reach out and find someone who believes in us and shares our vision so much that they will gladly and powerfully hold that vision for us. It is a privilege for them to do so and they know it.

Though your dreams may vary from mine, they all come from that same place. Your dreams are the gateway to your soul. It is the dream realized that sets your soul to dancing and it is the dance that matters; it is the dance that sets you free.

Remember, you did not come here to sit on the sidelines and watch. You came here to dance.

*I have written a piece entitled **"Will You"** which I share with you below. These words personify for me what it means to have the honor of holding a dream for another person.*

TODAY, I WISH FOR YOU TO HAVE SOMEONE IN YOUR LIFE, WHO WOULD BE WILLING TO ANSWER YES, TO THE FOLLOWING QUESTIONS:

Will you see me in the way I want to be, and not the way I am now?

Will you shelter my dream, hold it close, and give it life?

Will you feel my desire, and claim it, as your own truth?

Will you embrace what is real for me when I am lost in this illusion of fear and doubt?

Will you believe in me, especially when I can't, or won't, believe in myself?

Will you catch sight of my triumph, as you go about your day, and smile for me?

Will you hold onto my dream, when I am tired and weary, and I've almost given up?

Will you cradle my heart, when it is about to break, and give it back to me, healed and whole?

Will you never waiver, never falter, never tremble?

Will you cushion the blow, when I fall down, and can't get up?

Will you imagine me bigger than I am, greater than I am, grander than I am?

Will you enfold me in the magic, in the wonder, in the miracle of it all?

Will you summon the angels when things get in the way?

Will you make room for both of us, in the quiet meditations of your own mind?

Will you appreciate how far I've come, and, how close I am?

Will you keep the faith, even when the outer circumstances of my life, seem bleak?

Will you remember nothing is impossible and remind me?

Will you be the one who refuses to listen to my excuses, my ramblings, my doubts?

Will you celebrate my small victories along the way?

Will you refuse to allow me to give up, no matter what?

Will you lead me home to myself and help me see that I had it all the time?

Will you play with me, like children making up their life?

Will you ensure I don't take any of this for granted?

Will you behold me, resplendent in my success, and giddy in my victory?

Will you?

Is there a person in your life for whom you would like to hold a vision? Perhaps you could empower each other.

DAY 14 - CREATE SOMETHING TODAY

TODAY, I WISH FOR YOU TO CREATE SOMETHING.

A poem, a blog post, a handmade card, a painting, a song, a soufflé, a software application.

The form is unimportant, only the passion matters, and the calling of your own spirit to the aliveness of BEING in this moment.

Seek not perfection and release all judgment.

Simply put your heart into it.

Stamp your name upon it, imbue it with love, and PRESENT it to the world.

It matters more than you know.

Then celebrate it.

Celebrate you.

Celebrate the life that gave it to you.

C'mon... We're waiting!

DAY 15 - CAPTURED BY MIRACLES AND OVERTAKEN WITH JOY

TODAY, I WISH FOR YOU TO BE CAPTURED BY MIRACLES AND OVERTAKEN WITH JOY.

Let MIRACLES sneak into your life while your back is turned, and JOY seep into your being when you're not looking and overtake you.

Let your HEART disclose the answers to the questions you have been searching for while you were gazing the other way.

Let the INSIGHTS on the other side of your mind tug at your core and their divine messages whisper into your tender-hearted ears.

Let your BODY tell you what it

wants to experience, to dare, to excel at, to overcome, to encounter, and to rejoice and delight in.

Let your FINGERS write or type or play what they've been wanting to reveal but you haven't allowed them because you've been too busy or preoccupied.

Let your EYES see in spite of the darkness that surrounds you when they are closed and shut.

Let the SILENCE awaken truths locked away and unveil hidden meanings in the simplest of things.

Set your EMOTIONS free, let your feelings dance, feel the sensations surface and ignite.

Let the PASSION deep inside you bubble up and burst forth into the biggest, brightest smile and let it erase any sadness, grief, or anger that may still be lurking there.

Let your LAUGHTER emerge in the most unusual ways and in the most unexpected places and uplift those lost and disillusioned souls who share your path.

Let your day be captured by miracles and overtaken with JOY.

DAY 16 - WHAT DO WE REALLY KNOW FOR SURE?

The other day something happened that shook me up; something shocking and unexpected and perplexing. It made me doubt certain things I had believed to be real and made me question my own truths. So, I asked myself what is it I do KNOW for sure at this point in my life and I came up with the following:

WHAT DO I KNOW?

I know gratitude will fill my bank account faster than a New York minute.

I know a good cup of tea can solve almost every problem, and if not solve it, at least soothe it for a little while.

I know people need love more than they need things, but things are often how they get love.

I know when I focus with clear intention and absolute determination, I always get what I want.

I know there isn't any right or wrong, only what my own heart is telling me.

I know laughter and sunshine restore my soul.

I know the sight of a freshly opened morning glory makes my heart sing.

I know nothing is more fun than playing with a puppy, except perhaps playing with a dolphin.

I know time by myself each day makes me easier to live with.

I know the more I learn, the more humble I become.

I know it's the simple things in life that bring me joy and I can choose to be happy for no reason.

I know life circumstances change and that may be a good thing, even if it doesn't appear to be at the time.

I know out of great sadness and despair, joy will come, if I just surrender and let go.

I know everything tastes better outside.

I know pansies are extremely deceiving. They're much stronger and hardier than they look and so am I.

I know freedom is an inside job.

I know love is the only thing we take with us when we leave.

Today, I wish for you to ask yourself what it is YOU truly KNOW with every fiber of your being, at this point in your life right now.

I would love to hear from you. If you like, you can share your answers by emailing me here: veronicamhay@gmail.com

*Or leave a comment at the **Today, I Wish For You - BLOG** at this link: www.todayiwishforyou.com*

DAY 17 - SEEK JOY TODAY AND ALLOW YOURSELF TO FEEL GOOD

TODAY, I WISH FOR YOU TO LET JOY BE A BIGGER PART OF YOUR LIFE. SEEK IT OUT.

Look for it in the cracks, in the crevices, in every little nook and cranny.

Immerse yourself in its wonder. Feel its power and light embrace all that you are. See it coming around hallways and opening doors for you.

Play with it, cajole it, caress it. Surrender to its impulses. Succumb to its temptations.

It won't steer you wrong or lead you astray. Walk with it, talk with it. Allow it to show you the way. Make it real for you.

It wants to show you what is possible. It can bless and heal your body in ways you had not imagined.

It sleeps inside you. Awaken it. It knows the secrets deep within, the ones you are not aware of yet.

Persuade it to tickle your fancy, pinch your funny bone, restore peace and ease to your day.

Share it with those you come into contact with, even the ones that annoy you.

It will clear the path to riches and mend your broken heart.

It gently whispers ancient truths into your beckoning ears, and you will begin to understand the purpose of all your pain, especially in these troubling times.

It is your friend, your confidant, your long lost love, returning home again to claim your heart.

Welcome it in NOW!

DAY 18 - ARE YOU LETTING PROSPERITY IN?

TODAY, I WISH FOR YOU TO KNOW WHEN YOU ARE LETTING PROSPERITY INTO YOUR LIFE. HERE ARE TEN WAYS.

1. I know I am letting prosperity in when I can be on the receiving end of someone's anger, see only fear in their heart, and respond with love.

2. I know I am letting prosperity in when I make conscious choices during the day to focus on what it is I am wanting to create in that moment, or what it is I am desiring to be or feel or experience in this here and now.

3. I know I am letting prosperity in when I choose to clear myself of

some of the "guck" in the form of frustration, disappointment, or worry, that shows up occasionally throughout my day. After I take the time to do that, in the many and varied ways that are available to me, I always feel lighter, clearer and more at peace.

4. I know I am letting prosperity in when I am able to sit in the same place I did a week ago, a month ago, a year ago, witness the incredible abundance all around me, and bask in the multitude of treasures that had eluded me before. They were always there, but I didn't have the eyes to see them, from the place I was standing in at the time.

5. I know I am letting prosperity in when I feel more expansive, more open; when I can look at what appears to be a setback and acknowledge that, in the bigger picture, this could be a blessing in disguise, and remember several times in my life when I was so happy that things didn't turn out quite as I had wanted them to.

6. I know I am letting prosperity in when I am in any situation, a crowded city bus, a grocery store with long check-out lines, a traffic jam, and still experience joy, knowing that wherever I go I walk among the gods, in whatever setting we have chosen, and whatever costumes we may be wearing today.

7. I know I am letting prosperity in when I begin to savor the ordinary events in my day, the ones I so often took for granted before, as trivial and unimportant, the same ones I now embrace with rapture in my heart. I forget not, what life would be without them. I have not, the luxury to do that anymore.

8. I know I am letting prosperity in when I recognize things are not always as they seem and I am willing to look at any circumstance in another way. I know true prosperity can be experienced with the tiniest shift in perception. It truly is an inside job. We take ourselves with us wherever we go.

9. I know I am not letting prosperity in when the desire to get even or to be right takes over and I give in to it. Sometimes, there is a momentary deliciousness in this indulgence, I have to admit. In these

moments I can laugh at myself, have compassion for my humanity and see it for what it is. I notice my behavior and make a different choice the next time, and if it's a better choice, I acknowledge how much I've grown in the process.

10. I know I am finally and completely letting prosperity in when my world looks upside down, when the foundations of my life are shaken, when nothing seems to make sense anymore, and I can be at peace with all of that. *(P.S. I am not always there yet for this one.)*

DAY 19 - BEGIN TO REMEMBER WHO YOU REALLY ARE

TODAY, I WISH:

Remember who you really are ...

That you take some time to close your eyes and IMAGINE and DREAM, so big and so deep, that you become like the caterpillar that emerges as the butterfly.

That you LAUGH today, harder than you have ever laughed before, so hard, that your sides ache, and tears stream down your beautiful, glistening face.

That you LEARN something new today, a truth so utterly amazing, that it shakes you up, and rocks your world.

That you SAVOR the little things in your day today, such as your first cup of coffee, snuggling with your puppy, your baby's sighs, or your loved one's embrace.

That you SMELL one magnificent flower, so near and so intensely, that your nose rejoices to be a part of such an extraordinary face.

That you SEE, truly see your own soul reflected in someone else's eyes, and you don't run away, even though you'd like to.

That you WALK today, with a firm step, and a confident stride, as if you are going somewhere, because you are.

That you PRETEND you are rich and witty and wise; whatever it is you are wanting to be, act as if, pretend to be that now.

That you FORGIVE everyone who has hurt you, and you understand the deeper purpose of all your pain.

That you TASTE everything in your life today, the food, the wine, the rain drops, the snow flakes, each other, with your eyes closed, and your senses fully open.

That you PLAY today, with all the innocence and abandon of a sweet child, unaware of anything else, but this precious moment.

That you ALLOW yourself to, BE today, what your heart calls you to be, and DO only those things that bring joy to your spirit.

That you TELL the truth, and keep your word, and judge no man.

That you FORGET today, forget your age, forget your past, forget your aches and pains.

That you begin to REMEMBER, who you really are, and why you came here, and how very much you are loved.

DAY 20 - HOW MANY WAYS TO DIE, MY LOVE?

TODAY, I WISH FOR YOU, THE GIFT OF LIFE.

It is never too late to start living, to take one step forward and reach for our dreams. Perhaps reading this piece may inspire you to do just that.

I ran into a dear old friend recently whom I hadn't seen or spoken to in many years. We sat together for a while and talked about our lives and reminisced about times gone by. He spoke mainly of regrets and unrealized dreams. The passion I had seen in his fiery blue eyes all those years ago was gone; the light had gone out.

I felt deeply saddened as I watched him walk away slowly, his step without purpose, his body weary. He was still living and breathing, but no longer fully alive and I found myself thinking these words as he disappeared into the distance:

HOW MANY WAYS TO DIE, MY LOVE?

Every time we stop believing we can.

Every time we deny who we really are, or what we truly could be.

Like owning a mansion and opening the front door, but never going inside any of the other rooms, for fear of what we might find there.

How sad there are no funerals for the walking dead. No corpse to bury. No tears to shed.

No final moment of glory. No words of comfort that could stir us onto life... at last.

How do we recognize each other?

By what we have in common.

A book unwritten, a song unsung, a play unplayed.

A child unborn, a world unseen.

A love not given, or worse not taken.

So many miscarriages, never a birth.

So many excuses, never a reason.

Often our path in life is like a walk through a graveyard, on a summer's day, it feels warm and cozy, but its dead there.

How much longer before we wake up?

Some of us die a thousand times each day, remembering not to live.

How many ways to die, My Love?

Far too many, indeed.

How many ways to live, My Love?

Only One... Passionately!

DAY 21 - TO SEE THE WORLD WITH NEW EYES

TODAY, I WISH FOR YOU TO SEE THE WORLD WITH NEW EYES.

As you have never seen it before, like an alien on an unfamiliar planet, and not take anything for granted.

I wish for you to spend more time in nature, not on the path near your home, with its cell phones and incessant chatter, but deep in a forest, where the earth recognizes your step, and the ground kisses your feet as you walk.

I wish for you to say 'no' more often, and not feel guilty, and say 'yes' more often, and not feel embarrassed.

I wish for you to eat your spaghetti with a fork; forget about the spoon and get your face really dirty.

I wish for you to get to know your teddy bear, your cat, or your dog. After all, they have always been there for you, in your darkest hour, comforting you and whispering sweet messages into your heart.

I wish for you to speak or write more about those things that matter to you, with passion, that which you know in your gut, the things that fire up your life.

I wish for you to sit with a flower and watch it bloom, and know what it feels like to surrender to life, to succumb to a purpose bigger than your own.

I wish for you to speak to the moon and bask in the sun and gaze at the stars for hours and hours.

I wish for you to love more, not the sappy, greeting card kind of love they sell on Valentine's Day cards, but a love that surpasses all distance, time, space, and differences.

I wish for you to make friends with those parts of you that you are afraid of and attempt to do what still scares you to death.

I wish for you to break open the windows of your life and knock down the doors, remove the shackles, and stare down the illusion until it sets you free.

DAY 22 - THINGS I APPRECIATE ABOUT MYSELF

TODAY, I WISH FOR YOU, THE GIFT OF SELF COMPASSION AND APPRECIATION.

 "The art of appreciation begins with self-appreciation."

— AMIT ABRAHAM

Taking time to acknowledge ourselves and those things we value about who we are and what we have accomplished is so important. It is paramount in learning to love ourselves and then to open our heart to love others. It is not only essential. It is life changing.

So today, I am asking you to acknowledge yourself and the things you are proud of, those moments in your life when you knew in your heart of hearts you made a real difference in this world. I am sure there are a lot more of them than you realize and doing this process will help to bring them to light so you can celebrate them, celebrate you, celebrate life.

Below is my list. I hope it may inspire you to come up with your own.

THINGS I APPRECIATE ABOUT MYSELF

I appreciate my creativity and resourcefulness; they have kept me in the game and made me proud even when it felt like I was David and the world was Goliath.

I appreciate my delicious sense of wonder and childlike innocence and the fact that I love teddy bears and puppy dogs and pizza.

I appreciate that I am an uplifter and an inspiration to others and there are people on the planet still alive today because of something I said.

I appreciate that I am uniquely human and magnificently divine and some days I can't even tell the difference.

I appreciate all of my setbacks and failures along the way; I learned from them and see them all as blessings in disguise.

I appreciate when my parents died, I thought I would too, but I didn't.

I appreciate that I feel deeply and by allowing myself to move through the greatest pain I could then experience the deepest joy right on the other side.

I appreciate that I didn't always get what I asked for, but I always got what I really needed.

I appreciate my incredible sense of humor and my natural propensity to laugh easily and heartily with others or even all alone.

I appreciate my strong will and those people who told me something couldn't be done. They made me determined enough to prove them wrong.

I appreciate my sensitivity; there were times when I cursed it and times when I blessed it and times when I gave it away.

I appreciate my sense of style and love of beautiful things and my ability to take the ordinary and make it extraordinary.

I appreciate my capacity to recognize the angels in my life, the ones dressed in silk and the ones covered in fur.

I appreciate that I am amazing and brilliant and awesome and remarkable and humble enough to know so are you.

I appreciate me, with all my faults and foibles; there has never been, nor will there ever be, anyone quite like me, and that is reason enough to truly love who I am, and I finally do.

Now, it's your turn. What do you appreciate about yourself?

If you like, you can share your answers with me here: veronicamhay@gmail.com

Or leave a comment at the Today, I Wish For You - BLOG at this link: www.todayiwishforyou.com

DAY 23 - DECLARATION FOR FREE MONEY

TODAY, I WISH FOR YOU:

*The Gift of **FREE MONEY** requested in the form of the following declaration, command, edict, or decree, or whatever you would like to call it. Please say it to yourself silently or out loud, with heart, as if you mean every word, in this moment or anytime you wish to experience more money in your life.*

FREE MONEY

I desire free money and lots of it.

Not money I have to work hard for, struggle to receive or justify in some way.

Not money that is borrowed, manipulated, controlled, or coerced.

FREE MONEY

No contracts or agreements said or unsaid.

No constraints or conditions, read or unread.

A plethora of money freely given, for no reason, no purpose, no strings attached.

The answer to my greatest prayer. Much like air, it's always there.

FREE MONEY

I invite it into my life like a long lost lover come home again to steal my heart.

I welcome it into my world as a cherished guest at the sweetest tea party of my life.

A profusion of money, a cornucopia of abundance, an avalanche of prosperity.

FREE MONEY

I accept no excuses. I surrender all blocks. I release all barriers. I overcome all obstacles. I abandon all payoffs.

I embrace possibility, befriend magic, encourage change, seek wonder, salute joy.

I dream a new dream, walk a new walk, talk a new talk, write a new script, speak in a new, clear, and articulate voice.

FREE MONEY

I give up control. I relinquish need. I focus. I allow. I let go. I get out of my own way.

I embrace it wholeheartedly, no holding back, no pretenses, no games.

I will court it, romance it, engage it, persuade it, even serenade it, until I have won its heart.

FREE MONEY

Delicious, delectable, delightful, deliriously happy money.

It is my birthright, my inheritance, my legacy.

I declare it, demand it and deem it mine - NOW!

DAY 24 - IMAGINATION - THE GENIE INSIDE YOUR MIND

TODAY, I WISH FOR YOU, THE GIFT OF IMAGINATION.

One of the greatest gifts we have been given is our imagination. It costs nothing to access, is available 24/7, and is our doorway to freedom.

With imagination, we have inside of us the most amazing ability to change our state and transform our lives in a moment.

With imagination, we can experience whatever we desire, dream any dream, uncover the secrets of our heart, awaken our inner longings, and live them here and now.

With imagination, we have the freedom to choose the details of our world and see them come alive right before our very eyes.

With imagination, we are transported to any place, time, event, outcome, or circumstance we wish to explore. With the flicker of our eyelids, we can become anything we want to be and do anything we want to do.

With imagination, boundaries disappear, limitations cease to exist, and the impossible becomes possible.

With imagination, passions ignite, talents explode, and our abilities expand and magnify.

Imagination is the genie inside your mind, waiting to be let out.

Our body doesn't know the difference between this so-called reality we live in and our imaginings. It responds the same way to both. The secret to success with imagination is in the feelings. We need to feel, deeply feel, our way to happiness or love or whatever it is we are wanting. We must engage all of our senses to such a degree that when we open our eyes once again, we are surprised to be here. If we do this often enough, one day we won't be surprised. We'll be living the life of our dreams.

So, dear heart, what will you imagine today?

DAY 25 - GIVE UP THE SHOULDS, THE COULDS, THE WOULDS

TODAY, I WISH THAT YOU DON'T GIVE ANY THOUGHT TO WHAT YOU SHOULD DO. DON'T PAY ANY ATTENTION TO WHAT YOU COULD DO. DON'T DWELL ON WHAT YOU NORMALLY WOULD DO.

Instead, throw out the shoulds and the coulds and the woulds and do something totally different, something you have never done before.

Something unique, remarkable, exciting, sweet, inspiring, unfamiliar, awesome, carefree, surprising, crazy, impossible, fun, amazing, thrilling, unrealistic, or even silly.

Something that calls you by name, and beckons to you to come out and play.

Something that still scares you and the thought of it makes you weak in the knees, causes your heart to flutter and your mind and brain to wake up and take notice.

Something that makes you feel awake, alive, ageless, vibrant, victorious, indestructible, and undaunted. Something that fills you with passion, meaning, exuberance and joie de vivre.

Something you'll remember fondly for many days to come with a huge smile on your face and a twinkle in your eye every time you think of it.

Something that gives you that warm and fuzzy feeling inside, with no expectation, no purpose, no rhyme or reason, other than the sheer joy and aliveness of being.

Something nourishing to your body and delightful to your spirit, something that inspires your cells to get up and dance like nobody's watching.

Do that one thing today, perhaps trembling, but moving forward. One step at a time, one moment at a time, one breath at a time.

Begin! Do It NOW!

(P.S. You're doing it for all of us! So, thank you for your courage.)

DAY 26 - BECOME A SILENT ANGEL

TODAY, I WISH FOR YOU TO ANSWER YOUR SOUL'S CALLING AND TAKE THE HIGHER ROAD, BY BECOMING A SILENT ANGEL FOR SOMEONE ELSE, OFFERING RANDOM ACTS OF KINDNESS WHEREVER YOU GO.

Be on the lookout for places you could shine your light on someone else's darkness.

Be constantly aware of where your wings may take you, whether it be to a busy shopping mall, a lonely sidewalk cafe, a homeless shelter, a park bench, or a dinner party.

Be continually vigil of where you could look beyond the surface to the deeper pain that is lurking there and attend to it in whatever ways and means may lie before you.

Pretend you have been given a mission and you are part of the "silent angel invasion" of whatever city you live in or visit and it is your job to heal the minds and hearts of those you encounter along the way.

Sounds daunting? Fear not! You have at your command an arsenal of tools with which to do your work, a magic wand you can point and shoot better than any camera will ever do and grant silent wishes to unsuspecting, troubled hearts, uplifting them and restoring peace on earth.

A big, beautiful, heart full of love, with light beams that extend from you for miles and miles ahead washing away any sadness in the distance and replacing it with joy, wonder, belief in the magic, and trust in the knowing; we are all in this together.

We as silent angels have the ability to recognize each other. A knowing glance, a curious nod, a gentle, sweet, and innocent touch. A sacred salute to a comrade-in-arms and wings and halos.

So, dear heart, will YOU join me? Will you take your place among us? Will I sense you standing next to me wherever I may journey?

I know I will, for I feel you here, reading these words, and I already recognize you.

DAY 27 - TAKING TEA AT THREE O'CLOCK

What enchants you and gladdens your heart?

Perhaps it is looking into the eyes of your golden retriever as you stroke her soft, fur lined body, or sneaking out to an afternoon matinee and giggling in the back seat, in the dark, with your best friend and a tub of buttered popcorn, or working in your garden and letting the sweet smell of the earth transport your senses and the flowers caress your being.

Whatever it may be for you, it is important to capture those feelings of aliveness and exhilaration and let them take you to that place of absolute joy!

For me, a daily custom that brings me much pleasure is afternoon tea, which I have written about below.

TAKING TEA AT THREE O'CLOCK

> "Think what a better world it would be if we all, the whole world, had cookies and milk about three o'clock every afternoon and then lay down with our blankets for a nap."
>
> Robert Fulghum - From All I Really Need To Know I Learned In Kindergarten

I have always been moved by the above words by Robert Fulghum, about the importance of daily ritual and connection in our lives.

I once read a story of a lady who worked for a design company in New York, and every day at exactly three o'clock, a formal tea was served for all their employees.

How wonderful that must have been. A tea party in the middle of the afternoon at work!

I have enjoyed afternoon tea in so many delightful tea rooms and hotels, the most memorable being high tea at the Banff Springs Hotel in Alberta, Canada, overlooking a breathtaking view of the Rocky Mountains. It was a truly regal experience.

Taking tea for me is a form of meditation. A moment to sit in solitude and ponder life's meaning, or a time to connect with others in a comforting way. I swear we have solved most of the world's problems, my friends and I, armed with a big pot of tea, some serious scones and heated conversation.

There is a lot to be said for taking some time each day to do something that makes us feel good. I love the act of ceremony in a tea party. The beautiful cups and saucers. The enchanting teapots. The tinkling sound of the teaspoons. The tea bubbles on top of the cup when the tea is poured just right. The delicious tea sandwiches daintily made.

It always seemed to me there is nothing so bad that a good cup of tea could not fix, and if not actually fix, then soothe for a little while.

So my dear friends, today at 3:00 PM (Mountain Time), I will be taking tea (as they say).

Will YOU join me?

To watch a silent 2-minute video of this piece visit: www.teaat3.com

DAY 28 - MORE PASSION IN YOUR LIFE

TODAY, I WISH FOR YOU TO ALLOW MORE PASSION IN YOUR LIFE.

> "The only people for me are the mad ones, the ones who are mad to live, mad to talk, mad to be saved, desirous of everything at the same time, the ones who never yawn or say a commonplace thing, but burn, burn, burn, like fabulous yellow roman candles exploding like spiders across the stars."
>
> — JACK KEROUAC

The secret ingredient to success in anything we do is to find the passion in it, the kind of passion that makes you bounce out of bed in the morning because you can't wait to begin your day. Many of us have lost our enthusiasm for life. We have settled along the way for getting by, surviving, making do with what we have, not expecting too much in case we're disappointed.

Some of us have completely given up on our dreams. In fact, we don't even

Passion

remember what those dreams were, deciding they were too out of reach, not worth the effort we think is necessary to make them come true. We have lost our passion for life, our reason for living. We have resolved ourselves to mediocrity and sold ourselves in the process.

I hope that reading the following piece about passion will stir up your life and ignite the fire within you. That fire may have died, but the light hasn't gone out. As long as you are alive and breathing, it never will. It is waiting there where you last left it. Can you remember where that was?

PASSION

The difference between a job and a career.

The difference between an actor and a star.

The difference between a song and symphony.

The difference between a painting and a work of art.

The difference between caring and intimacy.

The difference between romance and rapture.

The difference between intelligence and genius.

The difference between living and being alive.

Passion

Wanting to jump out of bed in the morning.

Wanting the night to never end.

Wanting the moonlight to last forever.

Wanting to reach and touch the sky.

Wanting forever to be longer.

Passion

When everything tastes like champagne.

When everything smells like freesia.

When everything looks like Christmas.

When everything sounds like Mozart.

When everything feels like velvet.

Passion

When heaven is not a place to go to, but a place to be.

When success is not a thing, but a feeling.

When love is not an offer, but an acceptance.

When music is not a sound, but a resonance.

When life is not an existence, but a celebration.

DAY 29 - THE POWER OF NOW - A PROFOUND MOMENT OF AWAKENING

TODAY, I WISH FOR YOU, THE POWER OF NOW, AND A PROFOUND MOMENT OF AWAKENING.

(Please take some time to be alone and contemplate these words.)

May you rest here in this moment of now, allowing in all the possibilities that lie before you and letting go of any perceived encumbrances, trials, or tribulations.

May you pause here, welcoming all the guidance and support that awaits you, and releasing all that no longer serves you in any way.

May you bask here, taking in fully all the freshness that sustains and nourishes you, and dissolving all that has become weary and too difficult to hold.

Let it all go, let it melt away, vanish, and disappear.

You are here now, in this moment, which unfolds before you like a flower.

And like a flower, nothing is asked of you, but that you be real, authentic, and true.

And like a flower, nothing is required of you, but that you are present, awake and profoundly alive.

And like a flower, nothing is demanded of you, but that you be open, willing, daring, conscious.

May this moment be blessed with the gifts of insight, understanding, compassion and a deep inner knowing.

May the grandest mysteries of life beckon to you, and may you yield to their advances and surrender to their affections.

May you ask of life that it take from you whatever it may so that your place here has purpose and your journey be not in vain.

May you take the time to cease the inner chatter and feel the stillness in your own soul, and in that stillness may you see with new eyes, the perfection of each being in your life and the gifts they lay before you at your feet. May you gladly embrace those gifts and take them into your gentle and opening heart.

This time is sacred, as is every moment lived from a conscious place.

May you be accompanied by angels, precious beings from all places and times holy, and seen and unseen friends, who quietly rejoice alongside you in your awakening; those beings who want only the best for you and see you in your splendor, even when you do not.

When you are done with this moment, may you enfold it in love and send it into the world where it will uplift the planet, touching each person in a profound yet almost imperceptible way, like a butterfly alights upon a flower, aware of something forever changed.

For every time you breathe a little lighter, the world is lighter, and the healing begins for all of us; not just for some of us, but for all of us.

When you have the courage to awaken, you do it for everyone, because you are everyone.

DAY 30 - MAKE A WISH

TODAY, TIME FOR YOUR WISH...

Make a WISH for someone else today.

(Don't tell them about it.)

Sprinkle it with stardust.

Wrap it in gossamer wings.

Drizzle it with fairy dust.

Splash it with golden love.

Let it be sun-kissed and heart-felt.

Wave it a tender goodbye.

Send it softly on its way.

See it moving through the universe, knowing that it will be bringing tears of joy to the recipient.

It is all because of YOU.

You are that powerful.

You matter.

You can change the world.

One person and one wish at a time.

Close your eyes and DO IT NOW!

BONUS DAY 31 - BELIEVE

For those months in the year that have an extra day in them.

TODAY, I WISH FOR YOU TO JUST... BELIEVE.

Believe in the magic, even if you can't see it yet.

Seek enchantment, allow wonder, discover the grandeur, feel the presence, receive the grace, let in the rapture, romance the mystery, be open to possibility, touch the triumph, caress the splendor, embrace the love, seize the moment.

Trust, know, imagine, investigate, seek out.

Surrender, release, dare, captivate, connect.

Visit the forest with the tiny cottage and twinkling lights. Call forth the ancient ones who wait there for you. Gather the angels and unseen friends around you, more numerous than before. Invite the fairies, elves, gnomes and kindred spirits.

The little tree will disclose its secrets. The river will gift you its message. The cavern will tell you its story. The mountain will shelter your dreams. The firelight will awaken your spirit. The truth will tug at your soul.

'Tis a place of magic. Go within, be still, listen. Tread lightly, walk softly, whisper.

Explore this land, inside and out. Where obstacles cease, troubles melt away, struggles show themselves as lies, hardships flounder, worries disappear, turmoil dissolves, and pain evaporates.

Rest in knowing miracles are the order of the day.

Kindness and generosity abound and laughter captures your heart. Age doesn't matter, differences don't exist, time stands still.

Believe... Believe... Believe...

Believe in a pristine new world, right around the corner, waiting. YOU are the creator, producer, inventor, architect, and mastermind.

Never stop believing. Don't think of giving up. You've come too far. Help is on the way. Hope looms tall and strong. Passion is at hand. Joy waits in the shadows. Happiness is a given. Peace comes dressed in miracles.

Life begins again, greater than before.

Take bigger steps.

Breathe larger breaths.

Sigh louder sighs and believe.

Just BELIEVE.

CHRISTMAS BONUS - MY HOLIDAY WISH FOR YOU

THIS HOLIDAY SEASON, I WISH.

That you take time to smell the holly, the pine trees, the poinsettias and the chestnuts roasting.

That you hear, really hear the words of the beautiful, Christmas carols.

That you feel the snow beneath your feet if you are lucky enough to have it.

That you wonder at the reflection of the Christmas tree lights, the starlight, the moonlight, glistening across the land.

That you see enchantment in a small child's face on Christmas day, and that part of you comes alive again too, if only for the moment.

That you ride a Christmas sleigh and build a snowman or snowoman.

That you don't get too tired or too irritated with the shopping.

That you remember, it's the thought that counts.

That you allow people to love you, hug you, kiss you, and you don't get too embarrassed.

That you give thanks for everything you have been given, and you remember the lonely, the sad, the isolated, and you know that your smile may make a difference to someone else's Christmas, someone who may be feeling lost, because a person whom they loved very much, won't be with them this year.

That you call that friend you haven't spoken to in years.

That you tell your secretary, wife, husband, lover, how you couldn't get along without them.

That you buy yourself a special Christmas present because you deserve it, and no one knows better than you, what you have always longed for in your heart of hearts.

That you light a candle, and hug your dog, stroke your cat, and feed your fish.

That you remember to remember the feeling of Christmas long after it is over, long after you open your Christmas bills, and wonder what you've done, and was it worth it. Because it was, you know.

That you still believe in Santa Claus, angels, Christmas elves, miracles, love, laughter, peace, and joy on earth because if enough of us believe, they just might happen.

Then, little by little, Christmas may last longer and longer, and the world will be that much more beautiful because YOU are in it.

Merry Christmas

AFTERWORD

Dear Reader

I hope you enjoyed your time here and, in some way, your heart was touched and your spirits lifted, and that your life will be better for that.

Please let me know what your favorite wishes were from this book or tell me about your very own wishes for the day, at the **Today, I Wish For You - BLOG** at this link: www.todayiwishforyou.com or email me directly at: veronicamhay@ gmail.com.

I wish you Godspeed on your journey, my dear and precious friend.

Love and blessings, Veronica

SUBSCRIBE TO INSIGHTS AND INSPIRATIONS

and receive instant access to our guided audio meditation entitled *Gifts From The Soul.*

Each day you will receive an inspirational piece designed to uplift, inform, encourage, support and inspire you for the day.

Here is the link: http://geni.us/72kv

A FINAL QUOTE

Your dreams are the gateway to your soul.
It is the dream realized that sets your soul to dancing,
and it is the dance that matters, it is the dance that sets you free.

Remember ...
you did not come here to sit on the sidelines and watch.
... You came here to dance! ~ Veronica Hay

follow your dreams

Made in the USA
Middletown, DE
23 April 2018